American History Arts & Crafts

LEARNING ABOUT THE
CIVIL WAR
WITH ARTS & CRAFTS

Kira Freed

PowerKiDS press.

New York

Published in 2015 by **The Rosen Publishing Group, Inc.**
29 East 21st Street, New York, NY 10010

Library of Congress Cataloging-in-Publication-Data

Freed, Kira.
 Learning about the Civil War with arts & crafts / Kira Freed.
   pages cm. — (American history arts & crafts)
 Includes index.
ISBN 978-1-4777-5871-7 (pbk.)
ISBN 978-1-4777-5874-8 (6 pack)
ISBN 978-1-4777-5867-0 (library binding)
1. United States—History—Civil War, 1861-1865—Study and teaching—Activity programs—
Juvenile literature. I. Title. II. Title: Learning about the Civil War with arts and crafts.
 E468.F86 2015
 973.7—dc23

                                    2014033928

Copyright © 2015 by The Rosen Publishing Group, Inc.

Developed and produced for Rosen by BlueAppleWorks Inc.
Art Director: T. J. Choleva
Managing Editor for BlueAppleWorks: Melissa McClellan
Photo Research: Jane Reid
Editor: Marcia Abramson
Craft Consultant: Jerrie McClellan

Photo & Illustration Credits:
Cover, p. 22 top, 26–27 justasc/Shutterstock; cover side images (top Jose Gil/Shutterstock, middle Timmary/Shutterstock,
bottom Winslow Homer/Public Domain); title page, p. 8–9, 14–15, 20–21, 24–25 Austen Photography; sidebars Kletr/
Shutterstock; boxes foxie/Shutterstock; p. 4 map Rainer Lesniewski/Shutterstock; p. 4–5, 6 right, 12–13, 12 left, 13, 13
right, 22, 23, 26 left, 27 right, 28 left Library of Congress/Public Domain; p. 5 left and right U.S. National Archives and
Records Administration/Public Domain; p. 5 map National Atlas of the United States/Public Domain; p. 6–7, 28 top
Detroit Publishing Co./Library of Congress/Public Domain; p. 6 left, 7 right Mary A. Livermore/Public Domain; p. 7 left
Public Domain; p. 8 left Winslow Homer/Public Domain; p. 10 top U.S. Navy/Public Domain; p. 10 Andrew J. Russell/
Library of Congress/Public Domain; p. 10 right J.B. Elliott/Library of Congress/Public Domain; p. 11 Jo Davidson/Louis
Prang & Co/Library of Congress/Public Domain; p. 16 top, 26 top Alexander Gardner/Library of Congress/Public Domain;
p. 16 left L. Prang & Co.,/Library of Congress/Public Domain; p. 16 Arthur Eugene Preston/Shutterstock; p. 17 Thure de
Thulstrup/L. Prang & Co./Library of Congress/Public Domain; p. 18–19 Haas & Peale/Library of Congress/Public Domain;
p. 18 Max Smith/Public Domain; p. 19 right, 22 left, 23 left, 24 left, 26 right Mathew B. Brady/Library of Congress/Public
Domain; p. 20 left U.S. National Archives and Records Administration/Public Domain; p. 23 right H. B. Lindsley/Library
of Congress/Public Domain; p. 24 left James Gardner/Library of Congress/Public Domain; p. 27 left Alexander Hay
Ritchie/Library of Congress/Public Domain; p. 28 G. W. Thorne/Library of Congress/Public Domain; p. 28 right Carol M.
Highsmith's America, Library of Congress, Prints and Photographs Division; p. 29 right Department of Defense photo/
Public Domain

Manufactured in the United States of America

PSIA Compliance Information: Batch #CW15PK For Further Information contact: Rosen Publishing, New York, New York at 1-800-237-9932

Table of Contents

North Against South

The Civil War is considered by many to be the greatest challenge ever faced by the United States. Disagreement over slavery and states' rights pitted North against South. The nation nearly broke apart and suffered deep losses.

The Mason-Dixon Line divided the North (free states) and South (slave states). Many people in the South grew crops on large farms called **plantations**. The free labor of slaves allowed plantation owners to grow rich. The North's **economy** was mainly based on factories that produced guns, clothing, and farm equipment.

DID YOU KNOW ?

A few states were in favor of slavery but not **secession**. Those states were called "border states." Located between the North and South, citizens of border states had a difficult time not taking sides.

Although Virginia voted to secede in the spring of 1861, many residents of the western part of the state wanted to remain with the Union. As a result, West Virginia became a new U.S. state.

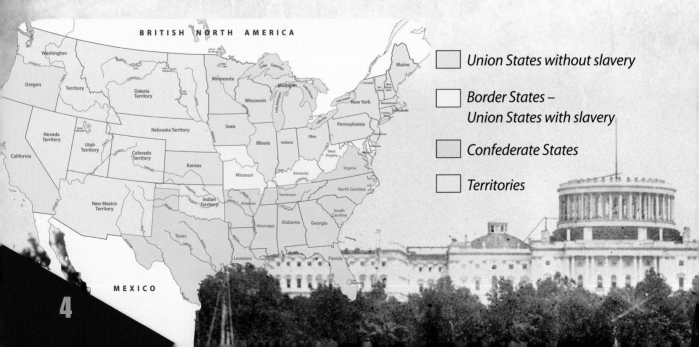

Union States without slavery

Border States –
Union States with slavery

Confederate States

Territories

The Issue of Slavery

The North and South strongly disagreed about slavery. By 1860, all Northern states had laws outlawing slavery. Many white people in the South defended slavery and feared that the anti-slavery movement would destroy their way of life. They also felt that individual states, not the U.S. government, should decide whether to allow slavery.

Abraham Lincoln was elected president in November 1860. Before he took office, seven states in the South left, or seceded from, the Union (the United States). Those states formed their own country, the Confederate States of America, and elected Jefferson Davis as their president.

The Mason-Dixon Line divided the North from the South.

Abraham Lincoln – President of the Union

Jefferson Davis – President of the Confederacy

5

The Fight Begins

Fort Sumter was located in the harbor of Charleston, South Carolina. After South Carolina seceded on December 20, 1860, its governor wanted the fort taken back from the U.S. government. President Lincoln refused to turn over Fort Sumter. In response, Confederate soldiers fired on the fort for 34 hours beginning on April 12, 1861.

DID YOU KNOW?

Abraham Lincoln did not want the country to split apart and tried to resolve the conflict peacefully. He thought slavery was wrong but did not want to force the South to end it. Instead, he said he would not allow slavery to spread to new territories and states. Lincoln's position on slavery made Southerners fear that, as president, he would put an end to it. When he was elected in 1860, he won without the support of any Southern states.

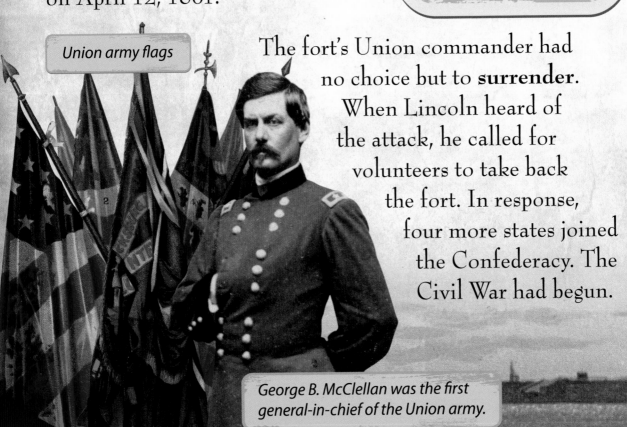

Union army flags

The fort's Union commander had no choice but to **surrender**. When Lincoln heard of the attack, he called for volunteers to take back the fort. In response, four more states joined the Confederacy. The Civil War had begun.

George B. McClellan was the first general-in-chief of the Union army.

First Battles

Confederate soldiers, called "Rebels," were excited by their victory at Fort Sumter. Union soldiers, or "Yankees," responding to Lincoln's call to reunite the country, marched toward the Confederacy's capital at Richmond, Virginia. They planned to attack a railroad center near Richmond on July 16, 1861. People from Washington, D.C., came to watch the First Battle of Bull Run as if it were entertainment. They expected a quick win for the Union, but instead its army was crushed. After several more Confederate victories, the Rebels felt confident they would win the war.

General Robert E. Lee commanded the Confederate army.

GENERAL ROBERT E. LEE

In April 1861, a U.S. Army general offered Virginian Robert E. Lee the opportunity to command the Union army. Lee opposed secession, but he was more loyal to his home state than to the Union. After learning that Virginia had seceded, Lee returned home and accepted a command in the Confederate army. His most important position was commander of the Army of Northern Virginia.

Confederate army flags

Craft to Make:
Zouave Fez

Typical Civil War uniforms were blue for Union and gray for Confederate, but many other uniforms were also worn, especially early in the war. The uniforms of recklessly brave soldiers in the French army, called Zouaves, were popular among some military companies on both sides. The uniform consisted of brightly colored baggy trousers, a short blue jacket, and a fez hat or turban. Close to one hundred companies wore the Zouave-style uniform. The last Union soldier killed in battle in Virginia was reportedly a member of a Zouave unit.

Zouave-style uniforms were more colorful than other Civil War uniforms.

What You Will Need

- Red felt
- Ruler
- Scissors
- Yarn
- Tapestry needle
- Glue, white and clear
- Cardboard
- Button

Step One

Measure an 8-inch (20.3 cm) square piece of felt.
Cut the corners off to create a circle. Measure and
cut out of felt a rectangle 5 inches (12.7 cm) wide
by 23 inches (58.4 cm) long.

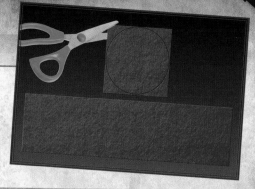

Step Two

Thread 24 inches (61 cm) of yarn on the needle.
Tie a knot at the end. Wrap the rectangle piece
around the circle. Insert your needle at the edge
of the rectangle and pull it through. Sew the circle
and rectangle together by stitching as shown in the
illustration. Overlap the rectangle slightly at the end.

Step Three

Turn the hat inside out so that your stitching
is now on the inside. Glue the overlapping
pieces of the rectangle together.

Step Four

Tie three 36-inch (91.4 cm) strands of yarn together
at one end. Braid the strands together and tie the other
end. Glue this to the top edge of the hat.

Step Five

Make a tassel for the hat. Cut a piece of cardboard the length
that you want the tassel to be. Wrap yarn around the cardboard
about 25 times. Cut the bottom of the tassel and then carefully
take it off the cardboard. Tie yarn around the top of the tassel
and knot it. Tie three 12-inch (30.5 cm) strands together.
Loop them through the top of the tassel. Braid the remainder
of the strand. Make a small hole with scissors in the top of the
hat. Pull the braid through and put the three strands through a
button and make a knot.

Naval Blockade

When Southern states seceded from the Union, Northern states stopped selling them supplies, including guns and bullets. The South hoped to get weapons and other goods by trading cotton to other countries. U.S. Army General Winfield Scott created a plan to send U.S. Navy ships to block **access** to Confederate ports. On April 19, 1861, President Lincoln ordered the **blockade** to prevent **foreign** ships from bringing supplies to the Confederacy. At first, only a few ships blocked Atlantic seaports, but as the Union's naval forces grew, ports on the Gulf of Mexico as well as large rivers were also blocked. The blockade lasted the entire war.

To get around the Union's blockade, the Confederacy used small, fast ships called blockade runners.

The blockade was part of the Anaconda Plan, named after a snake that kills by squeezing its victims so they can't breathe.

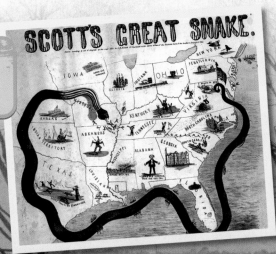

Ironclads *such as the* USS Onondaga *were powerful weapons in the Civil War. The era of wooden battleships was ending.*

Ironclad Ships

In 1861, Confederates recovered a sunken U.S. Navy ship, the *Merrimack*, off the coast of Virginia. Workers rebuilt the ship, covered it with iron plates, and renamed it the *Virginia*. The Union built its own ironclad, the *Monitor*. The two ships battled each other on March 9, 1862. Although they fired cannonballs and shells at each other for four hours, the iron plates proved to be effective barriers to serious damage, and neither ship won. The battle was the first between two ironclads. It marked the start of a new era in naval history.

DID YOU KNOW?

Submarines were new technology at the time of the Civil War. The Confederacy used submarines to attack blockading Union ships, while the U.S. Navy used them to clear Southern harbors of underwater obstacles.

The first sinking of a warship by an electrically detonated underwater mine, or torpedo, also took place during the Civil War. The ironclad USS *Cairo* sank in December 1862 after hitting a naval mine in Mississippi's Yazoo River.

The Confederate CSS Virginia *(left) fought the Union USS* Monitor *for four hours on March 9, 1862, in the Battle of Hampton Roads. The battle on Chesapeake Bay ended indecisively with both ironclads heading home for repairs.*

Slaves Turned Soldiers

Escaped slaves as well as free African Americans in the North wanted to fight against the South, but a 1792 law **prohibited** African Americans from carrying firearms in the U.S. Army. In addition, President Lincoln was concerned that border states would secede if the Union army had African American units.

Thousands of former slaves had settled in the North by 1860.

By the middle of 1862, however, the Union army was badly in need of soldiers because fewer white men were signing up. New laws made it possible for African Americans to enlist. Government posters began advertising freedom, pay, and protection to recently freed slaves if they joined.

African American soldiers made up about 10 percent of the Union army by the end of the Civil War.

Joining the Union Army

Recruitment of African Americans was slow until their leaders suggested that serving in the military was part of an effort to become full citizens. After that, more African American men enlisted. Many served at first in work **battalions** and volunteer units. Later on, the Union army had all-African American units. African American soldiers received less pay than white soldiers until June 1864, when an act of Congress granted equal pay.

In total, about 180,000 African American soldiers fought in the U.S. Army during the war. Close to 20,000 served in the U.S. Navy.

MILITARY ASSIGNMENTS

Confederate President Jefferson Davis was angered by the Union army's use of African American soldiers. He declared that all African American soldiers who were captured would be killed, as would their white commanding officers, or else sold into slavery. For this reason, many Union officials tried to keep African American soldiers away from the front lines. When they did fight in the front lines, African American soldiers were among the fiercest fighters in the war.

African American soldiers were fierce fighters.

Not every soldier was assigned to combat duties. Thousands of men served as clerks, quartermasters, cooks, medical staff, engineers, chaplains, scouts, spies, carpenters, laborers, and signal corps members.

Signal Lantern

Although it was dangerous, many slaves ran away from their owners beginning long before the Civil War. These freedom seekers tried to reach locations where slavery was illegal, including free states and Canada. They received help from people in the **abolitionist** movement, which was an effort to end slavery in the United States. Abolitionists included white people who detested slavery, former slaves, and free African Americans in the North. These people formed a network of help for escaping slaves called the Underground Railroad. Like a real railroad, this network had "conductors" (helpers), "freight" or "**cargo**" (escaped slaves), "stations" (safe houses), and "lines" (routes). Conductors sometimes used lanterns to signal that a station was safe to approach.

What You Will Need

- Empty can
- Paper and marker
- Tape and scissors
- Cornmeal or dirt
- Old towel
- Hammer and nails
- Wire and wire cutter
- Tea light candle

Step One

Clean your tin can. Cut a piece of paper the same size as your can. Draw a pattern of dots on the paper. Leave at least one inch at the bottom free of pattern. (If you put holes near the bottom of the can, wax might seep out as the candle melts.) Tape the paper to the can.

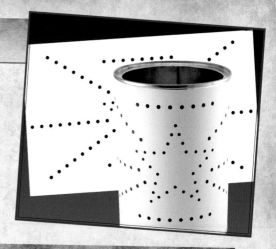

Step Two

Fill your can half full with dirt or cornmeal (this keeps the bottom from bulging out when the water freezes). Fill the rest of the can with water. Put your can in the freezer for at least 12 hours to freeze the water.

Step Three

Prepare a work area with an old towel, a hammer, and a variety of nails. Place the can on its side. Hammer a nail into all the pattern dots (not too far, just enough to make a hole). Use different size nails to create different size holes. Be careful not to hit your fingers. Make two extra holes close to the top edge on opposite sides of each other.

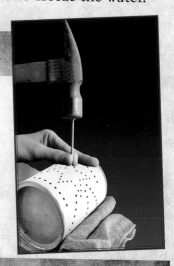

Step Four

Put the can in the sink and let the ice melt a little. Discard the frozen cornmeal or dirt. Rinse the can and let it dry. Have an adult cut a piece of wire. Put each end through the holes at the top and bend a little bit of the wire up to hold it. Repeat with the other side. Place a tea light candle in it and have an adult light it.

The Turning Point

Although the Union lost several early battles, it stopped Confederate forces from invading the North in September 1862 at the Battle of Antietam in Maryland. That victory created the **momentum** needed by President Lincoln to make a major announcement. In his Emancipation Proclamation, he declared that all slaves in states that were in rebellion against the Union would be freed as of January 1, 1863. Lincoln's announcement boosted Union **morale** and transformed its cause into a **crusade** for freedom. When slaves in the South heard about the Emancipation Proclamation, many found a way to join Union forces. Others simply rejoiced.

President Lincoln met with his generals at Antietam after the Union victory. This photo was taken in October 1862.

The Battle of Antietam is considered the "bloodiest one-day battle in American history." In 12 hours of fighting, an estimated 6,000 soldiers died and roughly 17,000 were wounded.

Gettysburg

Nine months after Antietam, in July 1863, Confederate forces again tried to bring the war to the North, this time in Pennsylvania. The two sides met at the small town of Gettysburg. A **brutal** fight raged for three days. The Battle of Gettysburg is considered the turning point in the war. The South's defeat and retreat back to Virginia ended Confederate hopes of invading the North.

The Battle of Gettysburg was the bloodiest battle of the war. Over 7,000 soldiers from both sides were killed, another 27,000 or more were wounded, and at least 10,000 were missing.

THE GETTYSBURG ADDRESS

Four months after the Battle of Gettysburg, President Lincoln spoke at the dedication of a Union cemetery near the site of the battle. His brief presentation, the Gettysburg Address, is one of the most famous speeches in American history. He reminded the nation of the principle of equality upon which the United States was founded. He also declared that the Civil War was a struggle both to keep the nation together and to bring equality to all its citizens.

This painting from 1887 shows Union forces at Gettysburg holding off a fierce attack known as Pickett's Charge.

17

Modern War

The staggering number of injuries and deaths was the result of changes in technology that caused the Civil War to be called the first modern war. Earlier long-barreled guns, called muskets, had **accurate** aim for only a short distance. Rifles, which were new, allowed soldiers to shoot ten times farther with accuracy. New cone-shaped lead bullets allowed for faster loading, as did new rifles that could be loaded from the back (called breech loading). Other weapons included repeating guns and new types of cannons. For protection from these new weapons, soldiers fought from trenches.

DID YOU KNOW?

In contrast to the many technological advances, medicine during the Civil War was primitive. Doctors had limited education and were rarely trained in treating gunshot wounds. Medical tests such as X-rays had not yet been developed. Most importantly, people at the time did not know about germs, so they didn't understand how to prevent or treat infections. About 200,000 Civil War soldiers died from enemy fire, and more than twice that number died from infections and disease.

The Gatling gun was a forerunner of the modern machine gun. It was first used in combat by the Union forces during the Civil War.

Other Developments

The Civil War saw the first use of the railroad to transport large numbers of troops and supplies. The Union had an advantage since it had more than double the mileage of the South's tracks. Another important invention, the telegraph, allowed President Lincoln to communicate in real time with Union officers. This device sent coded messages through electrical cables.

The Civil War was also the first war captured by cameras. The process, which was still new, required subjects to stand still for several minutes. Although no action shots were taken on the battlefield, many photos still captured the horror of the war's death and destruction.

OBSERVATION BALLOONS

Armies used observation balloons for the first time in the United States during the Civil War. The Union Army Balloon Corps was established in 1861. The *Union*, a tethered balloon filled with methane gas, was built soon after. Its purpose was to spy on Confederate troops near Washington, D.C. Knowing the location of enemy troops, Union guns could fire accurately without seeing them. Six other balloons were built soon after. The Confederacy also used balloons but with far less success.

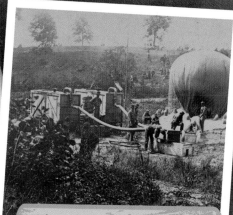

This photo shows Union balloonists using portable gas generators to inflate a balloon called the Intrepid.

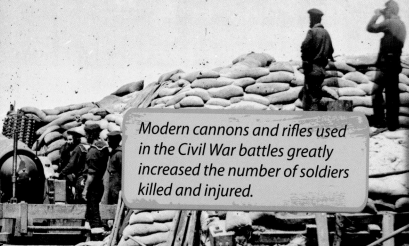

Modern cannons and rifles used in the Civil War battles greatly increased the number of soldiers killed and injured.

Craft to Make:

Army Drum

Union soldiers were required to be 18 years of age to enlist. For Confederate soldiers, the minimum enlistment age was 18 until 1864, when it was lowered to 17. Boys younger than the legal age could sign up as drummers. They played an important role, as the dozens of drumbeats they had to learn communicated different orders to troops.

Drummers played an important role in the army during parades, roll calls, and actual battles.

What You Will Need

- Hat box (you can purchase these at most craft stores or you can use an empty coffee container)
- Packing tape
- Paint and brush
- Cardboard
- Hole punch
- Double-sided tape
- Rope
- Carabiner

Step One

Tighly stretch the packing tape across the top of the box. Repeat this many times until the top is covered with at least two layers of tape. Wrap tape around the edge of the hat box for extra strength.

Step Two

Paint the hat box.

Measure the circumference of your hat box with a tape measure.

Cut two strips of cardboard from a discarded box. The strip should be 1 inch (2.5 cm) tall and as long as the circumference of the box. Paint these strips, or cover them in red duct tape.

Step Three

Punch 10 holes spaced evenly near the edge on the first strip. If your container is small, punch fewer holes. Repeat on the second strip but put the holes between where they are on the first strip. (You may need an adult's help punching holes if you use the duct tape.) Using double-sided tape, attach the strips to the hat box, making sure that the holes are above and below the edge of the hat box.

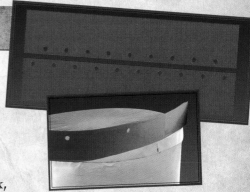

Step Four

Run thin rope through the holes of the strips alternating from top to bottom. At the end, tie the ends together and trim. If you would like to attach a strap for your drum, attach a carabiner to the side of the drum using several layers of tape.

Women at War

Before the Civil War, the lives of most white women revolved around home and family. After the war began, so many men were away fighting that these women had to take over many of their responsibilities. Many women worked on farms and in factories as well as in government jobs. Other women sewed, knitted, baked, canned, and grew fruits and vegetables for soldiers. Still others wanted to be more directly involved with the war. The North and South both had female spies, and over 400 women dressed as men and fought on the front lines.

Some women traveled with the armies. They helped with cooking, nursing, and laundry.

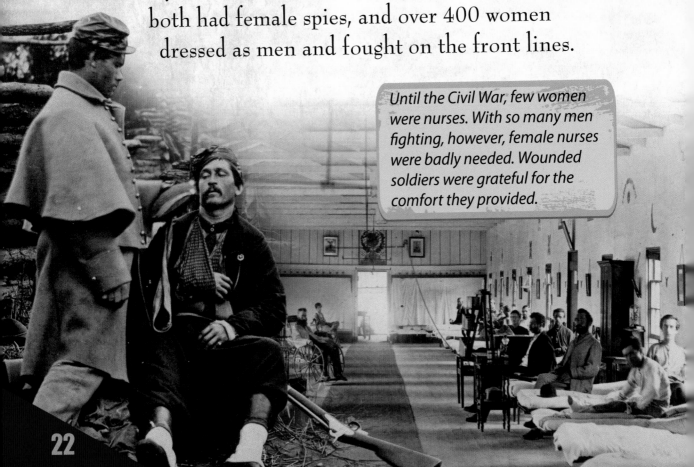

Until the Civil War, few women were nurses. With so many men fighting, however, female nurses were badly needed. Wounded soldiers were grateful for the comfort they provided.

The Angel of the Battlefield

Women also helped by serving as nurses. The most famous of these was Clara Barton. One week after the Civil War began, she left her job as a clerk to help injured Union troops. She collected food, clothing, medicine, and other supplies for them and asked friends to do the same. Before long, Barton set up an agency to distribute supplies, including to battlefields. She also tended the wounds of both Union and Confederate soldiers and earned the nickname "Angel of the Battlefield." After the war ended, she founded the American Red Cross.

Clara Barton was a Civil War nurse who founded the American Red Cross.

Harriet Tubman escaped slavery, then helped many others flee on the Underground Railroad.

Craft to Make:

Quilt Square

One way in which women supported the Union cause was by volunteering in the United States Sanitary Commission. This agency was formed to promote clean conditions and aid sick and wounded soldiers in Union army camps. It also helped soldiers who were returning from battles. Some volunteers worked in field hospitals, including as nurses and cooks. Others raised money, collected supplies, made uniforms, and performed other tasks. Many women made quilts at special events known as sanitary fairs. Over 200,000 quilts were sent to Union soldiers.

Members of the United States Sanitary Commission raised around $25 million to help soldiers wounded during the Civil War.

What You Will Need

- Thin cardboard or poster board
- Scissors
- Red, blue and white felt or construction paper
- Glue

Step One

Draw two 2-inch (5 cm) squares on the thin cardboard. Using scissors, cut them out.

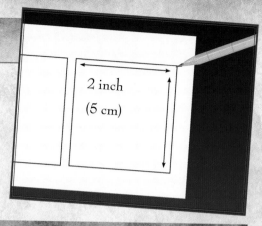

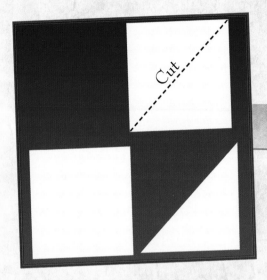

Step Two

Cut one of the squares from corner to corner to create two equal triangles. You will use the triangle and square as a pattern for cutting out the felt or construction paper.

Step Three

Using your pattern square as a guide, cut four squares out of one color of felt or construction paper for the center.

Cut four squares of the second color. Cut eight triangles of that color as well.

Cut eight triangles of the third color of felt or construction paper.

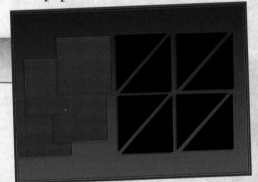

Step Four

Cut an 8-inch (20 cm) square out of felt or poster board to use as the base. Arrange your pieces on the base as shown. Lift each piece and apply glue to the base, and then place the piece on the glue and smooth down. Repeat for each piece.

Final Battles

Ulysses S. Grant commanded troops in the earliest important Union victories of the war. After other key victories, President Lincoln gave him command of all the Union armies in March 1864. Grant's goal was to attack nonstop to break the back of the Confederacy's armies. Several brutal battles took place that spring. Then, on Grant's order, General William Tecumseh Sherman's troops captured Atlanta, an important supply center for the Confederacy, in September. Several other Southern cities fell to the Union as well. The series of Union victories helped Lincoln win reelection in November.

Many soldiers on both sides died during the final battles of the war.

Ulysses S. Grant led the Union armies to victory over the Confederacy in the American Civil War. In 1869 he became the 18th President of the United States.

General Sherman was a skilled military tactician. In 1869 he became the Commanding General of the U.S. Army.

March to the Sea

Next, Sherman marched over 60,000 troops through the South, destroying every farm, road, bridge, and railroad line along their path. The goals were to wipe out Confederate routes and supplies as well as terrify people into giving up the Confederate cause. This "March to the Sea," along with Grant's victories in Virginia, crushed the Confederacy. General Lee had no choice but to admit defeat. On April 9, 1865, he surrendered the Army of Northern Virginia, which signaled that the South had given up hope of winning the war. Most of the other Confederate armies surrendered during the next month.

TERMS OF SURRENDER

Generals Lee and Grant met at the town of Appomattox Court House, Virginia, to discuss the terms of surrender. President Lincoln had already let Grant know that his foremost concerns were peace and reuniting the country, not **revenge**. Grant's terms of surrender were generous. Confederate troops had to give up all military weapons, but they could keep their horses and mules. Since many Confederate soldiers were near starvation, Grant gave them three days' worth of food.

The Confederate army surrendered on April 9, 1865.

Although it helped to win the war, the harshness of Sherman's "scorched earth" policy was often criticized.

Peace at Last

Five days after Lee surrendered, the United States flag was raised over Fort Sumter, where the Civil War had begun. President Lincoln and his wife went to Ford's Theatre in Washington, D.C., to see a play and celebrate the end of the war. During the play, a Confederate supporter named John Wilkes Booth shot Lincoln in the back of the head. Lincoln died the next morning. Millions of people honored the president as a train carried his body back to his home in Springfield, Illinois.

Fort Sumter marked the beginning and the end of the Civil War.

The train carrying President Lincoln's coffin stopped in 180 towns and cities so all Americans could pay their respects.

Visitors can see the gun that was used to shoot President Lincoln at Ford's Theatre, which is now a National Historic Site.

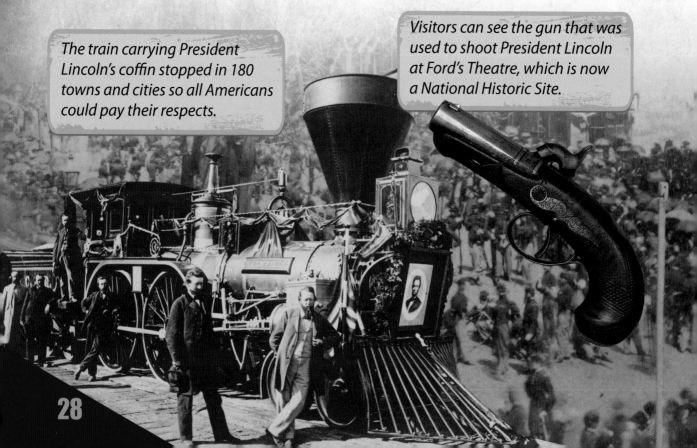

The Struggle Continues

After the Civil War, the United States became one nation again. Slavery was abolished, and new laws granted basic rights to African Americans. However, those gains were just a step in the struggle for equal rights. Many white people in the South strongly resisted the changes that resulted from the Civil War. **Segregation** laws, special tests and taxes for voting, and violence became their new tools for keeping African Americans from full equality. It took another 100 years before new laws in the 1960s created a stronger foundation of equal rights for every American. Although great progress has been made, more work is needed to bring about true unity and equality.

NEW LAWS

Three amendments to the U.S. Constitution became law soon after the Civil War ended. The Thirteenth Amendment (1865) abolished slavery. The Fourteenth Amendment (1868) established that all people born or naturalized in the United States, regardless of race, were citizens and prohibited states from limiting citizens' basic rights. The Fifteenth Amendment (1870) granted all men the right to vote, regardless of race, color, or previous enslavement. In addition, the Civil Rights Act of 1875 granted all citizens access to public places, regardless of race.

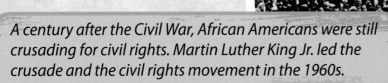

A century after the Civil War, African Americans were still crusading for civil rights. Martin Luther King Jr. led the crusade and the civil rights movement in the 1960s.

Glossary

abolitionist A person who worked to make slavery illegal.

access Permission or ability to get near, enter, or use.

accurate Able to produce a desired result or reach an intended target.

battalion(s) A large group of people, often soldiers, working together.

blockade An act of cutting off an area to keep people or supplies from coming or going.

brutal Extremely harsh, cruel, or violent.

cargo Goods that are transported.

crusade An organized effort to bring about change.

economy The resources and wealth of a region or country.

foreign Related to other countries.

ironclad A ship covered with iron plates.

momentum The force or strength that builds as a series of related events proceeds in a certain direction.

morale The confidence and enthusiasm of a person or group.

plantation(s) A large farm worked by many laborers.

prohibited Banned; forbade; made illegal.

revenge The act of punishing to get even.

secession The act of formally withdrawing.

segregation A policy that forces people of different races to stay separate in a certain location.

surrender To give up power, control, or ownership.

For More Information

Further Reading

Doeden, Matt. *The Civil War: An Interactive History Adventure.* You Choose Books/Capstone, 2009.

Rosenberg, Aaron. *The Civil War.* Scholastic, 2011.

Stanchak, John. *Eyewitness Civil War.* DK Publishing, 2011.

Websites

Due to the changing nature of Internet links, PowerKids Press has developed an online list of websites related to the subject of this book. This site is updated regularly. Please use this link to access the list: **www.powerkidslinks.com/ahac/civwa**

Index